Pathways and Passages

A Year of Haiku

Robert W. Barker

iUniverse, Inc.
Bloomington

Pathways and Passages
A Year of Haiku

Copyright © by Robert W. Barker.

The views expressed in this work are solely those of the author and do not necessarily reflect the views of the publisher, and the publisher hereby disclaims any responsibility for them.

iUniverse books may be ordered through booksellers or by contacting:

iUniverse
1663 Liberty Drive
Bloomington, IN 47403
www.iuniverse.com
1-800-Authors (1-800-288-4677)

Because of the dynamic nature of the Internet, any web addresses or links contained in this book may have changed since publication and may no longer be valid. The views expressed in this work are solely those of the author and do not necessarily reflect the views of the publisher, and the publisher hereby disclaims any responsibility for them.

Any people depicted in stock imagery provided by Thinkstock are models, and such images are being used for illustrative purposes only.

Certain stock imagery © Thinkstock.

ISBN: 978-1-4620-7244-6 (sc)
ISBN: 978-1-4620-7245-3 (e)

Printed in the United States of America

iUniverse rev. date: 12/29/2011

To Cynthia for love and patience.

To Robert for the first step.

To Zane for outstretched hands.

Forward

In the Spring of 2010 I embarked on the discipline of writing at least one haiku-style poem each day. The practice helped me to see my world, and sometimes myself, more clearly. One deeply personal result has been a growing, more peaceful sense of tolerance of the failures I see in myself and, of course, in all those who choose to navigate this world beside me. I am sorry to say that my tolerance still is far from perfect.

Though all of these poems are in essence statements of life relationships and change, I have loosely divided the book into four sections titled Relationships, Spirits, Nature and Vision, and ending with Pathways and Passages. Some of the poems, as is their nature, tend to defy classification.

I hope you will find some peace and enjoyment in these fifty-two poems from my year of haiku.

RELATIONSHIPS

Future runs to us,

Heart full of his tomorrow,

Consuming sorrow.

His arrival

Dark wind blows, sharply;

Evil invades his body,

Sowing its black seeds.

Cancer

Leave her quietly,

Carried in white ocean waves;

So many goodbyes.

The bed

These two are but one;

Bound, they stumble, walk again.

Can love be awkward?

Lasting love

Reaching my teacher,

The soul catcher, life changer,

We searched, together.

Martin, survivor

His head turns, he smiles;

Through his eyes I see my world.

His soul lives within.

My father

Forgotten in hate,

All those lovers who vanished.

No more love to heal.

Mosque protests

Turning, our friend smiles,

One last time, in departure.

Let the smile linger.

Lost friend

One day, you will come;

She spoke with great confidence.

Now, so old, she smiles.

Mrs. Bronson

It will rain again,

In our land of memories.

But sun also shines.

San Francisco, returning

I touch him lightly;

His skin covers sharp edged bones.

I am cold, afraid.

Sick friend

Stepping back in time,

Our world is forever, change;

Remembering youth.

Toronto together

SPIRITS

Reach high, touch the stars;
Naked, spirits visit me,
Ancient, enfolding.

Peru, Altiplano

Conflicted cultures,

Boundaries patrolled by ghosts,

Haunting all bridges.

Cultural gulfs

Down from the sages,
Stumble to the white salt plain;
It is a dream land.

Bonneville

Sunset, high Peru,

Distant peaks glow dark orange.

Old gods kiss this land.

Altiplano spirits

Ancient stone statues,
The gods stand in line, waiting.
Who worships them now?

Dead gods

Old Gods demand war.

Our Gods are too meddlesome.

Let us live in peace.

Muslim center, NYC

Touch the fading dreams;
Wind whispers, gray smoke dissolves.
Nothing left to hold.

911 anniversary

Windswept island speck,

Silent, gray, weathered buildings;

Fishermen's headstones.

Unga Island

Now but a shadow,

He lives in some other world,

And waits for passage.

Death struggle

Hold the bird lightly,

Tiny, fragile, beating heart;

Relax, let life fly.

Changes

NATURE
AND
VISION

Pink petals falling,

Magnolias young and thin,

Sentinels of Spring.

Vancouver Spring

Swimming, sharks seek prey;

Watching, I no longer hunt.

Peace demands no blood.

No longer the hunter

Gray mist blurs the point;

At low tide, pines touch dark rocks,

Caress the hardness.

Stanley Park

Piercing green, leaves reach;

Reaching back, across the gulf,

Our existence joined.

The joining

Long grass, gusting wind,

Green hills fade to distant peaks;

Time has lost this place.

Laramie

Clouds, glowing orange,

Bright against the eggshell blue;

Time forces darkness.

Ending day

Mountains bleed and fall;

Bones crash down the dark, bare cliffs.

We are intruders.

Mountain walls, Chile

Listen! Dogs barking,

Echoing conversations;

Announcing their pride.

Vanity

Dry, brown, brittle hills,

Cattle stand, in growing heat;

Where is the green grass?

Carlin

Her wings clip the light;

Perched, she turns her head, hunting.

Slips into darkness.

Owl

Clouds climb forest slopes;
Wispy birth in steep valleys,
Quiet leeward loss.

North Vancouver

Dry hills are burning,

Consuming life's vanities.

Tomorrow will be.

Boulder

Rain, falling gently,

Touching, measuring the land,

Flowing without time.

Winter rain

Burnished scythe of war,

Harvests screaming, bloody men.

The world lies starving.

Bitter harvest

Truth speaks, fearfully,
Unwanted, disfigured guest,
Hidden and denied.

Our times

We have lost the point,

Blurred in foggy confusion;

There, see it dimly.

Lost sea wall

PATHWAYS
AND
PASSAGES

The earth receives her,

Child of the earth returning,

Embraced, accepted.

Interment

Trees, thick, hide the path;

Look far, the forest guides you.

Losing, find your way.

Forest path

Searching for our path,

Time is the forest of life;

Listen to the heart.

Direction

Climb among giants,

Ancient mountains, dark blue sky;

We trespass, lightly.

Andean

Death creeps into life,
Quietly, with no fanfare.
Survivors embrace.

Comforting

Seeking your life's course,

The wise and fools can guide you.

Give value to fools.

Guidance

Secrets, long hidden,

Released at last with a sigh.

Acceptance granted.

Power denied

Time, signpost of life;

To gain life, leave time behind.

Treasure the losing.

The gaining

Shifting morning fog,

Obscures our close connections.

We all live alone.

Alone

Garden eternal,

Here we walk outside of time.

Yesterday is now.

Japanese tea garden

We tell old stories,

Not ready, yet, to grow old.

Caught between two lives.

Thanksgiving

The Queen's flag flies high;
She is home, in the palace.
The world passes by.

Buckingham Palace

Where is the young child,

Tearing at Christmas wrappings?

We are here, grown old.

After

Fierce intensity,

Heart of her creative life;

To her one last breath.

Author

One Ending

Another Beginning